VOLUNTARY ORGANIZATION AND SUSTAINABLE RURAL DEVELOPMENT IN MEGHALAYA

R. Gopalakrishnan
K.K. Jhujhunwala
A.K. Nongkinrih

2025
Regency Publications
A Division of
Astral International Pvt. Ltd.
New Delhi – 110 002

First Published, 2001

Reprinted, 2025

ISBN: 978-81-87498-29-2

Disclaimer:

Every possible effort has been made to ensure that the information contained in this book is accurate at the time of going to press, and the publisher and author cannot accept responsibility for any errors or omissions, however caused. No responsibility for loss or damage occasioned to any person acting, or refraining from action, as a result of the material in this publication can be accepted by the editor, the publisher or the author. The Publisher is not associated with any product or vendor mentioned in the book. The contents of this work are intended to further general scientific research, understanding and discussion only. Readers should consult with a specialist where appropriate.

Every effort has been made to trace the owners of copyright material used in this book, if any. The author and the publisher will be grateful for any omission brought to their notice for acknowledgment in the future editions of the book.

Published by : **Regency Publications**
A Division of
Astral International Pvt. Ltd.
– ISO 9001:2015 Certified Company –
4736/23, Ansari Road, Darya Ganj
New Delhi-110 002
Ph. 011A43549197, 23278134
E-mail: info@astralint.com
Website: www.astralint.com

Preface

PANACEA or Policy Alternatives for the North-East and Conflict Elimination Awareness is a Non-Governmental Organisation formed by people having more or less similar view points on the need and necessity of having sustained development in the North East. It was in the planning stage for nearly three years. It was registered as a society in May 2000. Its area of operation was Northeastern Region. It aimed at addressing itself to the economic and social relations. It emphasised upon the need to arrive at a conflict resolution that will ensure sustained development. In short, PANACEA essentially addresses conflict resolutions as a panacea for the problems in which the Northeast finds itself today these are Eco-spasms that combine environmental degradation at a large scale with continuous immigration, intense economic crises, social instability and violence.

Premises

The Northeast is characterized by very high population growth, continuous immigration, consequent demographic transformation, declining economic relations, rapidly increasing capital, technology and resource requirements, dwindling economic opportunities, worsening law and order situation and so on. Dissent was expressed as demand for a separate independent political status with insurgency-related activities as the means of expression. Marginal states like Meghalaya, Mizoram and Arunachal Pradesh displayed strains of regional compulsion. Rapidly growing working population in rural and urban areas became frustrated aggressive and hyperactive. They believed that both the state and the society at large owed them a wage and a place. This increased the levels of disaffection in the region as in Manipur, Tripura etc. Ethnic and political power became the focus of mobilization. Various levels of discrimination and deprivation emerged. This enhanced alienation and antagonism and was exploited by cross-border influences.

Objectives

- To promote an understanding of regional and ethnic diversity, pluralism and the need for peaceful co-existence.
- To analyze causes of disaffection among people and identify the problems that have led to it.
- To identify major trends in social, economic and political development and develop suitable strategies towards sustained development and conflict resolution in the northeast.

Challenges

Transformations in communication technology became visible initially as radio, wireless sets and telephones, followed by teleprinters and subsequently by copying machines, fax cellular phones, computer networking and other advanced communications like satellite communication facilities. National and regional level television networks cover much of the area. However, the peripheral areas of the region came under strong influences of Trans-border communication systems. Besides the availability of cable network, Internet facilities and extensive use of dish antennae have suddenly thrown the region wide open to external influences. These have introduced multiple and conflicting social, cultural and political messages. They have made development, politics of mass mobilization and the generation of popular consensus difficult. The divisive forces within and across the borders have continuously used these situations to challenge and subvert the power of the state. It is possible that without effective counter- measures, continuation and escalation of these instances may lead to a maelstrom of political violence—the ***turkification*** of the northeast.

Approach

The approach will be to direct effort to-

- Develop a coherent perspective at a broader local-regional level;
- Contribute to the formulation of strategies ensuring continuity in economic transition and development;

- Develop an understanding that will contribute towards mass-participation, thus encouraging the population to play a more pro-active role in restoring normalcy-inducing conditions.

Themes

Themes include:

- Identification of some of the aspects that have serious security and national concerns. This will include the nature and pattern of regional geopolitical impulses emanating from the adjoining countries of the northeast.
- Changing population composition and demographic transformations, their implications, responses and consequences.
- Problems of immigration and continuos infiltration and their consequences.
- Factors leading to increasing tendency of disaffection among population expressed through the rise of insurgency and related problems.
- Causes of low or stagnant economic growth.
- Electoral studies to reflect local needs regional perceptions and responses.

These will be carried out through projects (of short and long duration as well as individual and collective), seminars, symposia, working groups and so on).

PANACEA became an operational entity with the inauguration of a workshop entitled VOLUNTARY ORGANISATIONS AND SUSTAINABLE RURAL DEVELOPMENT IN MEGHALAYA between 28th and 30th June 2000 in Shillong. The workshop was well received by various participating NGOs, whose geographical representation included the West and East Khasi Hills districts, the Jaintia Hills district and the Ri-Bhoi district. The Shillong Urban Agglomeration was also well represented. The present volume is a report of this workshop. It is a summary of details of some of the participating NGOs as also the various problems faced by them. Despite various hurdles, these NGOs have kept the momentum and have continuously redoubled their efforts to contribute in concrete terms in the pre-dominantly rural areas of their development operations. They have been frequently handicapped by lack of financial resources and technological know-how. This workshop was aimed towards resolving these anomalies and provides the participants with information as to how they can successfully initiate development effort in their area.

The workshop was sponsored by the Council for Advancement of People's Action and Rural Development, (CAPART, Ministry of Rural Development, Government of India), New Delhi. Mr. Rangan Dutta, the Director-General of the CAPART, actively participated in the planning stage of the workshop. In fact, his participation ensured successful completion. We were able to take the benefit of experience and advice of Mr. Rangan Dutta and the CAPART Regional Office at Guwahati. Mr. K.B. Rani (Asst. Director, CAPART, NE Zone, Guwahati) provided information that was well appreciated by the participants.

This response from CAPART, was followed by the Chairperson of the Meghalaya State Social Welfare Advisory Board, General Secretary, Ka Lympung ki Seng Kenthai, and the Nehru Yuvak Kendra (all from Shillong). They explained the various schemes that were available for the NGO's to initiate development activities in their respective areas.

PANACEA is deeply indebted to Prof. R.C. Sharma, Visiting Professor Nagaland University, Lumami Campus, Mokokchung, Nagaland (who was the Chief Guest) to have taken a keen interest in the proceedings by providing a interesting inaugural address. This address not only explained the focus of PANACEA but also the need for development through NGO participation. Besides, Dr. K.K. Jhunjhunwalla, Dr. A.K. Nonkinrih and Father K. Paul along with Mr. Lakadr Syiem, Mr. K.K. Pariat and Ms Unimary Kharkongor, to name a few, channeled all their efforts to bring this workshop to a successful conclusion as well as summed up the expectations of the participating NGOs. This report is an expression of three days of debate and discussion.

This report was to be published within two months of the workshop. However, the delay in its publication has been partly due to administrative bottlenecks as well as the pre-occupations of the editors. The editors sincerely acknowledge the assistance and financial support extended by Mr. Rangan Dutta, Director-General, CAPART, New Delhi, without which the publication of this report would have been difficult, if not impossible. The editors are grateful to a host of people who, though unnamed have been indispensable. The editors express their gratitude to them. The editors also express their appreciation to Dr. N.P. Goel for word processing of the manuscript. The editors take full responsibility for errors and omissions in the report.

18th Oct. 2000
Shillong

Prof. R. Gopalakrishnan
Dr. K.K. Jhunjhunwala
Dr. A.K. Nongkinrih

Introduction

Meghalaya is situated in the northeastern region of India, between the Brahmaputra valley in the north and the Bangladesh in the south. It has a total geographical area of 22,489 Sq. Km. and is divided into seven administrative districts, two sub-divisions, six special administrative units and 30 community development blocks. It has a total population of 17.60 lakhs (1991 Census), with an average density of 78 persons per square kilometer. The average decennial growth rate of population was 32.30% (1981–91). More than 80% of the population lived in 4874 villages out of the 5044 recorded villages in the state. The state is characterised by agrarian economy. The level of development is low. Small scale industrial units along with cottage and handloom industries dominate the industrial landscape. Surface transportation, particularly the road transportation plays a vital role in the state's socio-economic activities.

Meghalaya Plateau has an elevation varying between 150m to 1961m above sea level. It is a heavily dissected terrain, particularly in the northern and western sides. Steep scarps or escarpments that fall abruptly to the Bangladesh plains dominate the southern side. The western part of the plateau or the Garo hills has an elevation of 600m above sea level. The most important relief feature of this part of the plateau is the Tura range with its highest point at Nokrek, 1515m above sea level. The central and the eastern part of the plateau or the Khasi and the Jaintia hills district play prominent senile topography. The central upland zone is the most important relief feature of the area and covers more than one-third of the area. It is east of the Garo hills. The highest point of this part of this plateau and that of the entire state is the Shillong Peak whose elevation is about 1961m above sea level. Escarpments mark the southern side of the plateau. It displays prominent erosional features. Cherrapunji and Mawsynram, located at close proximity to each other, have the heaviest rainfall in the world—more than 400 inches annually.

Soon after attaining statehood in January 1972, the United Khasi and Jaintia hills was divided; the Jowai sub-division was upgraded to form Jaintia hill district with Jowai as the district headquarters. Along with Khasi hills and Garo hills, this district formed the state of Meghalaya. In October 1976, the State Government issued a notification to divide the Khasi and Garo hills, into two districts each. The reason given for this division was administrative and developmental expediency. They were divided to form East and West Khasi hills districts and East and West Garo hills districts. In 1992, the West Garo Hills was further sub-divided into West Garo hills and South Garo hills districts, and, the East Khasi hills district into the Ri Bhoi and East Khasi hills district. The headquarters of these districts are as follows:

- i East Khasi Hills District—Shillong
- ii Ri Bhoi District—Nongpoh
- iii West Khasi Hills District—Nongstoin
- iv East Garo Hills District—William Nagar
- v West Garo Hills District—Tura
- vi South Garo Hills District—Baghmara
- vii Jaintia Hills District—Jowai

Subsequent to this, to effect greater administrative control and for management of development efforts, specific areas were created and designated as sub-divisions. These were:

(a) Jaintia border sub-division is renamed as Amlarem in the Jaintia hills district;

(b) Mairang sub-division including those areas of Mairang community development block that fell in the West Khasi hills district with Mairang as headquarters in the East Khasi hills district; and

In addition to these, following administrative sub units were also created. These were:

(i) Khliehriat including Khliehriat development block in the Jaintia hills district.

(ii) Sohra administrative area consisting of Shella- Bholaganj development block as well as parts of Pynursla and Mawsynram development blocks in the East Khasi hills district.

(iii) Mawkyrwat consisting of Mawkyrwat development block in West Khasi hills district.

(iv) Resubelpara administrative area consisting of seven gram-sevak circles in Resubelpara development block and parts of Dernbo-Rongsong community development blocks in the East Garo hills district.

(v) Dadengiri administrative unit consisting of three gramsevak circles in Resubelpara and Dadengiri community development blocks and Selsella community development blocks.

(vi) Betasing administrative unit consisting of Zikzak and Betasing community development blocks in the West Garo hills district.

Most interesting feature of the state is that the developmental planning is and has been carried out on the basis of the existing community development blocks. Till 1981, there were twenty-four development blocks. These were:

(a) Laskin community development block, Jaintia Hills
(b) Khliehriat community development block, Jaintia Hills
(c) Thadlaskein community development block, Jaintia Hills
(d) Bhoi community development block, Ri Bhoi
(e) Mawrynkneng community development block, East Khasi Hills
(f) Myliyum. Community development block, East Khasi Hills
(g) Mawphlang community development block, East Khasi Hills
(h) Pynursla community development block, East Khasi Hills
(i) Shella-Bholaganj community development block, East Khasi Hills
(j) Mawsynram community development block, East Khasi Hills
(k) Mairang community development block, West Khasi Hills
(l) Mawkyrwat community development block, West Khasi Hills
(m) Nongstoin community development block, West Khasi Hills
(n) Resubelpara community development block, East Garo Hills
(o) Dembo-Rongsong community development block, East Garo Hills
(p) Sonsak community development block, East Garo Hills
(q) Selsella community development block, West Garo Hills
(r) Dadengiri community development block, West Garo Hills
(s) Rangram community development block, West Garo Hills
(t) Zikzak community development block, West Garo Hills
(u) Dalu community development block, West Garo Hills
(v) Chokpot community development block, South Garo Hills

(w) Dambu-Aga community development block, South Garo Hills
(X) Betasing community development block, South Garo Hills

But there were many overlapping and difficulties in identifying the boundaries of the districts and community development blocks. However, these were ratified. Thus, instead of 24 development blocks, six more were created after 1981 for practical convenience Mairang east and Resubelpara west were treated as community development blocks along with Nongstoin, Khonjoy and Sonapahar. In other words, the six new community developmental blocks that were created after 1981 included: (a) Amalram community development block—from sub- division in the Jaintia hills districts. (b) New community development block included 14 villages of Mawrynkneng community development block and 55 villages of Pynursla development block. (c) Nongpoh community development block included 174 villages of the Bhoi area and 61 villages of Mairang development block. (d) Samanda development block consisting of lower portion of Songsak community development block in East Garo hills district. (e) Rongpara development block included areas east of Simsang River in Dambuk-Aga community development block in the West Garo hills district. (f) Mawshynreit (Sonapahar) development block included 220 villages of the Nongstoin-Sonapahar community development block in West Khasi hills district.

Thus from administrative and development point's of view, the state of Meghalaya was divided as follows:

During the period 1901–1991, the population of the state increased from 3,04,525 to 17,60,640 recording a population growth of +292.28%. The average decennial growth rate during this period was 32.04%. Broadly speaking, the population growth in the urban centres of the state was rapid. The population of the state is unevenly distributed and is determined by physiographic factors and accessibility. The population of the state is mainly concentrated in (i) the area around Shillong Urban Agglomeration, Jowai, Nongstoin, Williamnagar, Tura and Baghmara. (ii) The neighbourhood of Cherrapunji and Dawki, and (iii) Northern, western and southern fringes of the Garo hill.

The sparsely populated areas of the state are, therefore, found in the northern and southern Khasi hills, most of the Jaintia hills and the interior of the Garo hills. The average density of population in the state is about 78 persons per square kilometer. It is well below the national average of 267 persons per square kilometer (1991). The tribal component in the population is about 80% of the total population. In the interior locations of the state, like in the Mauzas of the Garo hills, the tribal component is often as high as 97%. However, in the peripheral parts of the state, the percentage of the total component in the population decreases. More than 40% of the non-tribal population of the state are concentrated in the urban areas and the rest are dispersed in the rural areas.

Percentage of literacy in the state is higher than the national average and stood at 33.35% in the 1991 Census. At the district level, the highest percentage is found in the East Khasi hills district with 41.10% and was followed by 32.28% in East Garo hills district, 30.95% in the West Khasi bills district, 25.44% in the West Garo hills district and 23.77% in the Jaintia hills districts. The percentage of literacy is highest in the urban centres, e.g. 62.92% in the Shillong Urban Agglomeration, 65.84% in Jowai and 58.01% in Tura. The state has also experienced in-migration of population.

The state of Meghalaya clearly illustrated variations in the proportions of working population and percentage of various categories of population to the total population. At the same time, the state also indicated a distinct trend between the urban and rural population structure. According to the 1991 Census, 71.96% were engaged in the primary sector, 11.82% in the secondary sector and 6.32% in the tertiary sector of the economy of the state.

Consideration of the Regional Environment of Meghalaya

With its level of economic development and complex social and political linkages, the state of Meghalaya is faced with immense and consequential environmental problems. Its prevention has become more of compulsion than a mere initiative in Meghalaya. This brief resume offers a reflection of national environmentalism with a concern to protect, preserve and provide remedial measures to the problems that have far reaching impact on the ecological stability of the areas at all levels of the scale. In this sense, such themes involve some accounting of how far and how well the awareness of environmental problems has advanced. It also includes the consideration of successes of the policy initiatives as well as the call for the blending of explanations with criticism at the appropriate levels. After independence, a concerted effort was launched to stabilise and accelerate the development in the country. Administrative reorganisation, inventory of resources, planning and identification of priority sectors were carried out side by side. Emphasis on sectors like agriculture, irrigation, power, transportation and communication industries and so on in the regional and national level economies encouraged the pace of development. The change and continuity resulted in optimism but compounded the environmental problems that emerged from growing population and rapid urbanisation. This was evident in the 1960's, when plans of the nineteen fifties gradually started materialising. These were coincident with large-scale deforestation and degradation through exploitation of needed building materials and fuels. Correspondingly, snags developed in the implementation levels as they passed through various administrative hierarchies. Conflict situations emerged as the policies confronting the traditional social-political structures in the various geographic regions of the state.

A step to accelerate the development has in its wake brought problems that had serious environmental connotations. These can be highlighted to include a) commercial exploitation of forests, economic development and consequent urbanisation, which has significantly accelerated the demand for timber within the state. In addition, with the presence of competitive markets in other parts of the country, the cutting of forests has proceeded at a faster pace than the natural replenishment of these resources. Correspondingly, efforts towards the afforestation likewise proceeded at a much slower pace. This had increased the area of deforestation. Further, increasing value of forest products, particularly timber has also added to the problem.

b) Shifting cultivation—this annually occupies an area of 530 Sq. Km of forest area with a minimum area of 2650 Sq. Km under jhum cultivation. Nearly 52,000 families are dependent on it, for their subsistence. This practice was congenial when the population density was low, forest area was abundant and the needs were limited. However, with the increase in population and economic develepment, this practice has triggered off series of negative effects. It's continuation has not only accelerated not only soil erosion and silting but also the loss of top soil, this made the surface barren and exposed the base rocks. This became useless for any future activity.

c) Urbanisation-changes in administrative status and subsequent administrative re-organisations followed by efforts towards diversification of the economy had significant impact on the environment.

Suffice it to say that new administrative units, community development blocks, forest circles and ranges and so on, had given adequate encouragement for new centres to emerge. These became focus of economic activities and became a cause of concern, from the stability of the environment in the respective areas. For example, rapid growths of Shillong Urban Agglomeration (and other district headquarters) have encouraged large-scale movement of population from both rural areas and outside the state. These were to a large extent in search of economic opportunities as well as due to urban center being the capital of the state. Service and tertiary activities developed at a rapid pace. As a result, there was a growing demand for construction materials, sites for location of establishments, etc. At the same time, issues like water supply, sewerage, disposal of garbage etc., assumed major significance. In short, these encroached on the forest areas. Besides, rapid growth of transportation and communication facilities and growth of small scale and service industries compounded the problems of the urban centres of the state,

Mining and Quarrying—Resource wise, the state is endowed with abundance of limestones, coal and other materials and construction materials in substantial quantities. Limestone and coal in particular occur near the surface and are largely located in the forested interior of the state. As a result, the process of mining in the state included removal of surface vegetation cover and the topsoil. The impact of this is obvious from the fact that on an average 4500 truck loads of coal from the state move daily to Guwahati. The movement of a fair percentage of timber for marketing outside the state has not only been an important revenue source but also one that provided meaningful employment to sizable section of people. However, with the legal suspension of felling of trees, a good proportion of work force has now found itself redundant. In the absence of any alternative occupation, this work force has assumed important connotations. The states as well as various traditional institutions, like wise, have yet to identify the alternative to compensate the loss of revenue. There has been an effort to review the decisions on felling of trees. Be that as it may, these only highlight the urgent need to identify and develop alternative economic activities/sectors that can provide the needed impetus for change and growth). The movements of these products through the roads and the urban centers have tremendously added to the vehicular pollution increasing the level of Carbon Monoxides and sulfur dioxide. Here is hardly any effort to fill up the pit mines or attempts towards afforestartion in these areas. Similar instances are noticeable in the limestone areas as well in the state.

Viewing these problems, one can think about the approaches available to minimise the impact of these activities. As noted earlier, there is no doubt that the costs of environment-stabilising approaches are very high. An effort therefore has to be made to incorporate the alternatives in the development perspectives and policies of the state. For example, the rapid depletion of forest cover in the state can effectively be tackled by regulation and enforcement's as well as by increasing the awareness of the benefits of the forests. The traditional societies of the state have in built institutional setups, e.g., by demarcating certain forest patches as sacred groves, of maintaining certain percentage of their respective territories under permanent forest cover. Although there are instances today of intrusion in these scared groves, efforts could be directed to strengthen these aspects of the traditional institutions and through them, progressively increase the area under forest cover while reserving other areas in a planned manner for commercial exploitation. Besides, the afforestartion clause should also be included as and when certain specified forest areas are earmarked for commercial exploitation. These alongwith other similar measures will go a long way in maintaining the ratio between forests and population.

As far as shifting cultivation is concerned, the development policies cold take into account local-regional needs and requirements of the populations. Alternatives through the capital inputs and locations of site-specific activities with minimum environmental hazards and effects could easily replace the existing pattern of selection. Moreover, the jhum control efforts could incorporate additional facilities that will increase the production and provide alternative opportunities.

There is an urgent need to control the urban pollution that is gradually transcending the urban spatial limits. Rapid increase in the construction of residential as well as commercial buildings, the quantum jump in the vehicular density, increasing emission of carbon monoxide and sulfur dioxide, near impossibility of expanding the existing road network and depletion of green cover within city limits, have all increased hazardous situation in the urban centers. Besides, proper drainage facilities and sewerage are hardly developed. Existing streams passing through the city are used both as source of water as well as for sewerage. Consequently, urban and industrial wastes have polluted the streams. They have also affected the areas through which the streams pass. Efforts have to be made to construct proper drainage-sewerage systems with outlet away from the urban center. Water and sewerage treatment plants could be incorporated so as to recycle the water before its supply for irrigation etc., while wastes obtained could be used as fertilisers.

As far as fuel is concerned, there is a distinct need to fine alternatives for wood. Substitutes for wood like quick maturing varieties can be grown in less favourable areas of the state. However abundance of forests in the state can be effectively used in this direction. As was suggested in a report from Delhi in the late 1970's, where the scientists used the pine needles for brequetting and found that they gave better energy ratios as compared to wood. Similar efforts in different vegetation situations can also be attempted to seek alternative fuel. Regarding mining and quarrying, it is better to adopt methods that leave the surface untouched. Efforts have to be made to produce more from the existing mines through pit mining.

On Economy

The state has an agrarian economy with more than 75% of the population, directly or indirectly dependent on agriculture. This percentage is concentrated on only 8.2% of the total geographical area of the state. The important crops of the state are potato, rice, maize, pineapple, banana and so on. Climatically, the region is an advantageous position as it favoured cultivation of crops, fruits and vegetables throughout the year. However, the rugged terrain had imposed serious limitations on this. As a result, the intensity of agricultural activity is very high in areas enjoying favourable conditions like in the Dadenggiri community development blocks in the East Garo hills, Mawphlang, Bhoi area and Mawrynkneng community development blocks in the East Khasi hills and Ri—Bhoi districts.

Animal husbandry and dairy farming are important; the state has 5.4 lakhs head of cattle, 29,000 buffaloes, 26,000 sheep's, 1.8 lakhs goats, 2.07 lakhs pigs and 14.19 lakhs birds in the poultry (1982 Agricultural census). The state also had the highest number high yielding crossbred cattle in the country.

The forest covers in the state are rich and extensive. Many of the existing locations of the forests in different parts of the state have been brought under reserved forests category today. They provide good quality timber and other forest products such as fodder grass, bamboo, firewood, etc. along with various medicinal plants and orchids. The state is also rich in mineral resources, particularly coal, limestone and sillimaninite. The state has a great potential for hydel development. However, per capita power consumption is far below the national average, i.e., 69 units as compared to 154 units of electricity. Yet, within the northeastern region, its consumption is the highest. Thus, out of the total energy generation of 1 155 million units in the region, the state's share was 367 million units and was second only to Assam.

Important industries in the state are confined to the manufacture of cement, plywood, a chemical factory, oil mills and so on. Almost all are of the medium scale industry. Other enterprises classified within the industries are sawmills, engineering units; flourmills, preservation units; sericulture, etc. come under the small-scale industry.

Roads are the main lines of transportation and infact the lifeline of the state. There are two national highways—one from the north to south via Guwahati to Shillong and extending upto the Bangladesh border and terminates at Tamabil—a distance of 155 Km; and the other from Shillong to Silchar via Jowai. It has an east to west orientation. This highway from Silchar in Assam extends to Aizawl in Mizoram and to Agartala in Tripura. Other important regional roads are Paikon-Bajendobe-Tura-Dalu-Baghmara road in the Garo hills and the Mendhipathar-PhulbariTura road. Besides these, Shillong-Jowai-Garampani road and the Shillong-Nongstoin-Tura road are also important.

The state has a total road length of 5,200 Km of which surface road length was only 2,761 Km. The density of the roads per 100 Km was 23.17 Km while 3.92 Km of road was available for every thousand population in the state. It is apparent that the high density of roads coincided with favourable relief and higher productivity and vice-versa. However, much of the state is dominated by difficult terrain and remained inaccessible; thereby reflecting low level of development.

Level of development in the state is low. Apart from Shillong and few other centres in the state, all other areas display the characteristics of backwardness and inaccessibility, in agriculture and industrial development. But by far the most important factor that has determined the developmental process in the state, has been accessibility pattern and availability of investable capital within the population of the state. Besides, the mountainous topography and the availability of suitable sites for carrying out economic activities had also exerted considerable influence. However, following are the main problems of economic development of the state, (i) Topography and imposed isolation are the limiting factors that inhibited growth; (ii) Location of major resources in relatively inaccessible areas; (iii) lack of market for capital goods followed by minimum interests in investments; (iv) high cost of transportation, and (v) Scattered nature of the exploitable resources and the relative geographical inertia combined to retard growth and development of the state.

Since 1987, efforts have been directed towards increasing the area under plantation of trees, though sustained afforestartion programmes, so that, area under Teak indicated plantation in 120 Ha in 1987–88. This increased to 140 Ha in 1988–89, to 200 Ha in 1991–92 and 225 Ha in 1995–96. Similar trends have been noticed in plantation of Sal from 220 Ha in 1987–88 to cover an area of 650 Ha in 1995–96, Pine from 150 Ha in 1987–88 to 740 Ha in 1995–96. Nearly 37% of the state is under vegetation cover. Of these, nearly 50% of the forest area is in the unclassed category and belong top either individuals or communal ownership. The rest comes under the control of the District Councils and the State Government. The State does not have a uniform land tenure system.

Despite the efforts for introducing more suitable varieties of rice, productivity of rice has declined at an average annual rate of 4.39 Kg per hectare in the last twenty-five years. Rice accounts for 78.38% (1,04,512 ha) of the total area under foodgrains (1,33,344 ha) in the mid-1990's. The decline in rice yields were off set by the HYV's of rice where the yields have been constant at 2, 300 kg/ha. This was against the overall average of 1138.71 kg/ha for traditional varieties of rice in the state (the traditional varieties of rice occupy nearly 65% of the total area under rice in the state).

Besides, most of the rice growing areas was located along the valley bottom areas. These areas are frequently subjected to flooding and deposition of silt and sand from higher slopes. Consequently, many of these areas are damaged and most of their standing crops destroyed seasonally and annually. These also damage the terrace fields, silting up of drainage channels and irrigation systems and so on. Another factor that has caused wide fluctuation in rice production is the erratic rainfall pattern during some years. Rainfall pattern during the period 1986 to 1996 has varied considerably and has compelled the need to resort to irrigation.

In the oilseed sector, Rape & Mustard which are largely grown in West and East Garo Hills Districts The area under Rape & Mustard in these districts has been gradually increasing (of the total area of 6632 Ha under Rape & Mustard, 5754 Ha (86.76%) was in West Garo Hills District, and 730 ha (11%) was in East Garo Hills District). There is adequate scope to increase the area under Rape & Mustard during the Rabi season in the state. Productivity increased at an annual average rate of 4.26 kg per hectare.

Sugarcane, Potato, Sweet potato, Tapioca and Tobacco are the important commercial crops grown in the state. Potato is the single most important commercial crop of the Shillong plateau—from Mawrynkneng village in the East Khasi Hills District to Nongstoin in the West Khasi Hills District. Potato was introduced very early in Khasi Hills during the British Period.

In order to strengthen the food grain sector of agriculture, efforts have been directed by the state towards the dissemination of modern technology applicable to small holdings in hilly terrain, Conversion of jhum land into permanent cultivated tracts, increasing area under High Yielding Varieties (HYV) of rice, wheat, maize, oilseeds, pulses and millets having resistance to diseases and pests, increasing double-cropped area through multiple cropping, adoption of short duration HYVs of rice to fit into the double/multiple cropping cycle, popularisation of the use of fertilizers, HYV seeds and need-based plant protection measures, and Integrated Pest Management, making available more numbers of power-tillers, tractors, power pumps and sprayers to farmers at subsidised rates, and dissemination of post-harvest technology to minimise post-harvest losses through pests and diseases.

Besides the state sponsored schemes like distribution of manure's and fertilisers at subsidised rates, there were Centrally Sponsored Schemes, (like Control of Pests and Diseases of Agricultural importance, Intensive Jute/Mesta Development Programme, Intensive Pulses development Programme, National Pulses Development Programme, Production and Supply of Quality Planting

Materials, Setting up of Integrated Pest Management Programme and Integrated Programme for Rice Development) and Externally-Aided Schemes/projects like Crop Husbandry, Commercial crop; Mushroom Processing Units, Tea Processing Units, Marketing & Quality Control Cold storage facilities for Agricultural produce and Expansion and modernisation of existing Fruit Processing Units) were implemented in the state.

Fibre Crops

Cotton, Mesta and Jute are important fibre crops and are concentrated in the Garo Hills sub-region of the State. Of these, Cotton and Mesta are Jhum Crops. Jute is grown as the second crop in paddy fields. These crops have been the traditional cash crops of Garo hills. The average annual area under Cotton was 7,460 Ha, with an average annual production of 4.280 bales at an average yield of 97.32 kg/ha. The average annual area under Mesta was about 5,500 Ha, with an average annual production of 22,580 bales at an average yield of 747.95 kg/ha, respectively. The average annual area under Jute was about 5,670 Ha, with an average annual production of 39,720 bales at an average yield of 1260.71 Kg/ha, respectively.

Spices

Varieties of spices are grown in Meghalaya, such as, turmeric, ginger, chilies, black pepper and bay leaf. Except for bay leaf, which is a forest product, the other spices are cultivated. The cultivation of turmeric (Lakadong variety) is concentrated in the Nongbah—Shangpung belt of Jaintia Hills District, while bay leaf is concentrated on the southern slopes adjoining Bangladesh. Chilies are grown all over the State while ginger cultivation is concentrated in East and West Garo Hills and East Khasi Hills Districts. Large cardamom has been introduced recently and is slowly becoming popular.

Plantation Crops

Arecanut, Rubber and Tea are important plantation crops. In recent year's coconut plantations is being introduced in a limited scale. Aeronaut cultivation has been introduced in an extensive scale in the northern slopes of Khasi Hills in the Ri-Bhoi district. A disease called Bud-Rot, which starts from the top and moves downwards, frequently afflicts this crop. Between 1971–72 to 1991–92, the area, production and productivity have been increasing at an annual average computed rate of 40 ha. 150 M.T. and 9.71 Kg/Ha.

Tea Experimental Stations were established at Umsning in Ri-Bhoi District (2.5 hectares), Riangdo in West Khasi Hills District (2.0 hectares) and Thebronggiri in West Garo Hills District (1.6 hectares) in 1976–77. Since then, the results have been encouraging and it was decided to grow tea as a homestead crop. In order to ensure the constant supply of good planting varieties, a Tea Nursery at Umsning in the Ri-Bhoi District and Rangram in the West Garo Hills District in 1982–83. To encourage the expansion of tea plantation in the state, several incentives, such as Cash subsidies of Rs. 12000.00 per hectare, released in five annual staggered installments, supply of plant protection materials like insecticides, fungicides etc., at 50% subsidy, and so on were provided. There is a private tea-processing unit at Sonapur. It processes green tea leaves from Umsning. At Rangram, local entrepreneur converts green tea leaves into finished product, which is mostly sold in the local market. At present, efforts are being made to accelerate the pace of expansion of area under Tea around both Umsning and Rangram, to achieve the production level to warrant the establishment of a mini tea-processing unit, at the earliest.

Meghalaya offers great potential for production of Mushrooms. A Regional Centre for Training and Production of Mushrooms in the Northeast was established in Shillong. The Centre is currently concentrating on the production and extension of (i) Agaricus spp. (White Button Mushroom) and (ii) Pleurotus spp. (Dhingri/Oyster). Of all the different mushrooms that can be grown by farmers, these two varieties have the strongest market Potential. Up till now, more than 700 farmers have been identified as trained growers and training sessions are being held regularly in villages in all the districts of the State.

Horticulture

Meghalaya is blessed with tropical, semitropical and temperate climates that permit the cultivation of a Wide variety of horticultural crops. The important horticultural crops currently being grown in the State are Banana, Oranges, Pineapple, Papaya, Jack fruit, Litchi, Plum, Peach, Pear, etc. At present around 9 per cent of the geographical area of the State is net sown area (1,98,000 ha) and the chances of adding new areas under agronomic crops are limited.

On the other hand, around 22 percent (4, 92,880 hectares) and 7.50 per cent (1,67,270 hectares) of the total reporting area of the state (22,39,000 hectares) are lying as Culturable Wasteland and Fallow land other than Current Fallow, respectively. In other words, the areas under these two categories (6,60,150 hectares) covers about 30 per cent of the total reporting area of the State, represents potential areas, in addition to the current area (30,000 ha) under Horticulture.

Pineapple, Citrus (Mandarin Orange) and Banana are most important Horticultural crops in the state. The average annual growth rate in production of all the horticultural crops is positive except Mandarin Orange which showed a negative trend 29.97 thousand MT In order to tap the horticulture potential, efforts have been directed to establish nurseries in all the districts of the state. These can be identified as follows:

No.	Location/Nursery (in Ha)	Area	Fruits & Plants
1.	**East Khasi Hills**		
	Fruit Garden Shillong	35.001	Plum, Peach, Pear, Naspati, Apricot and Chestnut
	Temperate Fruit Research Station Upper Shillong	6.00	Plum, Peach, Pear
	Horticulture Fruit Nursery, Wahjain	8.80	Litchi, Arecanut, Coconut, Orange, Assam lemon, Pineapple, Bay Leaf
	Horticulture Fruit Nursery, Pomshutia	8.00	Litchi, Arecanut, Coconut, Orange, Assam Lemon, Pinapple
2.	**Ri-Bhoi**		
	Pineapple Research Station, Dewlieh Umsning	10.00	Pineapple, Sweet Oranges, Naspati, Litchi
	Horticulture Fruit Nursery, Byrnihat	6.00	Banana, Pineapple, Guava, Black Pepper, Arecanut, Litchi, Assam Lemon, Coconut
3.	**West Khasi Hills**		
	Horticulture Fruit Nursery, Phodkylla	9.00	Orange, Arecanut, Coconut, Sweet Potato
4.	**Jaintia Hills**		
	Horticulture Fruit Nursery, Thadlaskein	10.00	Plum, Peach, Pear, Naspati

contd. . . .

contd. . . .

	Horticulture Fruit Nursery, Muktapur	3.00	Litchi, Arecanut, Orange, Assam Lemon
	Horticulture Fruit Nursery, Mynkre	10.00	Assam Lemon, Orange,
5	**East Garo Hills**		
	Horticulture Fruit Nursery, Sambrak	25.00	Orange, Coconut, Black Pepper, Litchi, Assam Lemon, Ginger, Turmeric
6	**South Garo Hills**		
	Horticulture Fruit Nursery, Mineng	8.00	Orange, Black Pepper, Arecanut, Cinnamon, Litchi, Grape fruit
7	**West Garo Hills**		
	Horticulture Fruit Nursery, Rangram	4.00	Orange, Arecanut, Cinnamon, Bay leaf, Large cardamom
	Horticulture Fruit Nursery, Zikzak	8.00	Orange, Arecanut, Bay Leaf, Litchi, Assam Lemon, Coconut
	Horticulture Fruit Nursery, Damalgiri	5.00	Orange, Arecanut, Litchi

N.B. In some of the above-noted farms vegetable seeds are also being multiplied.

Meghalaya is known for its vegetables in the region. Cabbage, cauliflower, radish, and squash are regularly marketed outside the State. The area, production and productivity in the vegetable sector have been showing an upward trend. In the base year 1978–79, the total area and production of vegetables was 4.66 ha. And 43.99 thousand MT, whereas the average for the 13 years period from 1978–79 through 1990–91 the area and production was 5.01 thousand hectares and 45.74 thousand MT and in 1990–91, 6.56 thousand hectares and 64.76 thousand MT, respectively. The most heartening thing in the vegetable sector is the rise in productivity in most vegetable crops. The extension of tomato cultivation during the last 3–4 years in the Umsning—Nongpoh belt deserves special mention. The farmers of this region are growing tomatoes in both the Wharf and Rabi seasons. The agro-climatic conditions in Meghalaya favour the cultivation of vegetables round the year. This climatic advantage is reflected in good prices fetched by vegetables when they are in off-season in neighbouring states. On the whole, the revenue return from vegetables tends to be higher than from cereals, and moreover, they can be grown in homesteads or on gentle slopes near the homesteads, facilitating the farmers to pay full attention to their care-maintenance regime. Corresponding developments were evident in fish seed production and distribution. This rose from 678200 units in 1991–92 to 1507000 unit's 1995–96, number of fish seed farms increased from 14 in 1991–92 to 16 in 1995–96. Nursery area declined from 3.2 Ha in 1991–92 to 2.3 Ha. in 1995–96 and Bhil and lakes from 375 Ha to 368 Ha. Number of villages under sericulture rose from 1469 in 1985–86 to 1812 in 1995–96.

Infrastructure

Fruit Processing-units

There are two existing fruit processing units in the State, one at Shillong in East Khasi Hills District with an installed capacity of 60 MT, and the other at Dainadubi in East Garo Hills District with an installed capacity of 40 MT. These factories manufacture Squashes, Canned fruits and juices, Jams, Jellies, Marmalade and Pickles. Apart from producing the conventional items like Orange Squash and Pineapple Jam, etc. these factories have recently started using indigenous fruits like Sohbrab (passion fruit), Sohiong (Prunus nepalensis) Soh Be] or Bael (Marmalades), Soh Pyrshong (Carombola), Soh Shang (Elacagnus sapida) and Soh Phie (Myrica nagi), to produce squashes, jam, pickles, etc. Recently Pineapple and Orange drinks packed in 200 m. RTS (ready-to-serve) packs have also been added to the list of items produced by these factories. These two factories form an integral part of the strategy for growth of the Horticultural sector in the state. They are equipped with state-of-the-art machines and manned by personnel trained at the various Food Technological Research Institutes.

Policies of Economic Development

Changing global economic linkages, rapidly interacting national economic situations, and local-regional level economic requirements and compulsions, induced parameters that needed immediate resolutions. As a consequence, the state reviewed its industrial and economic development policies and identified creation of employment opportunities in industry and allied sectors, development of human resource to aim at balanced growth oriented development with specific emphasis on promotion of village and small scale industries, creation of infrastructural facilities, industrial growth centres and industrial parks, identification of medium and large industries utilising local resources, encouragement to local entrepreneurship, promotion of local interests through joint ventures and promotion of high value—low volume products in view of transportational bottlenecks as priority sectors.

These were incorporated in the State's Industrial Policy of 1997. This policy also envisaged promotion and introduction of advanced technologies, external investments, and so on. Based on the available resources of the state, the Industrial Policy of 1997, aimed at encouraging the growth of Agro-Based Industries (like Horticulture based units, Bio-Technology based units, Tissue culture and Orchid units, Spice, Oleoresin and other essential oil units, Medicinal plants, Tea and Rubber), Animal Husbandry and Meat Processing Units, Development of Mineral based units (like Coal based units, Limestone based units such as cement plants, lime purification plants, calcium carbonate plants, Precipitated calcium carbonate units, Bleaching powder units, etc.,Other units such as Granite mining and polishing units, Sillimanite refractory and allied plants, Clay washeries, Ceremic glazed tiles, Ceramic crockery. Ceramic low-tension insulation) and Electronic and Information technology units in the state.

These units were to be encouraged by providing necessary infrastructural facilities, credit and finance subsidies, access to technology, relaxation in controls, better marketing strategies and so on. Besides, tourism was to be given adequate support, as it forms one of the few sectors in the State's economy that had the potential to provide more than adequate returns. Besides, there have been significant efforts to tap the Southeast Asian markets for export products, such as coal, lime stone, beetle leaf, handicrafts etc., (particularly with Bangladesh). The state's favourable agro-climatic conditions, provides the much required thresh hold point for accelerating economic growth. These prospects are enhanced by the location of the state in the wider regional environment. The latter, provides the required networks and linkages for such an effort

The above paragraphs clearly suggest that the Non-Governmental Organisations have ample scope to function and operate in the state. They can supplement the development effort and thereby induce economic development. It is in this context that the proceedings of the Voluntary Organisations and Sustainable rural development in Meghalaya have been presented.

Selected References

1. Government of Meghalaya, *Industrial Policy*, 1997.
2. *Review of Agriculture Meghalaya*, Department of Agriculture, Government of Meghalaya, Shillong, 1996.
3. A.K. Nongkinrih, *On Sustainable Development*, 1996. (Occasional Paper)
4. R. Gopalakrishnan, (2000) *Meghalaya, Land and People*, Revised Edition, Omsons, Guwahati and New Delhi. It is in this scenario that the Non-Governmental Organisations can function and operate in the state.

Chapter I

Meghalaya—people and Development

In any economic survey and assessment of the state of Meghalaya, parameters such as how well people are fed, their nutritional status, the average life expectancy, the infant mortality rate, the availability of sanitation, the availability of drinking water and its quality, the quantum of living space, the incidence of various diseases, dysfunctions, disorders or disabilities, access to medical facilities, literacy, the availability of schools and educational facilities, various levels of skills to cope with fast-changing economic and social demands and so on need to be elaborated. These are basic premises, whose status ultimately reflects the pace of economic change. One has also take into account the developments in the last five decades, particularly in terms of responses, representations and mobilisations in social and political relations to change. It also requires a fair assessment of the potentials as well as identification of the direction for the required changes, so that the obvious indicators of development, in the current parlance of the term, are wealth of the state, the prosperity of its people and the ability of the state to attract investment and technology. State Domestic Product (SDP), rate of economic growth, value of exploited resources, per capita income, credit and investment ratio, levels of savings etc., are some of the indicators of the wealth of the state. In addition, dynamism and strength of the economy, is reflected by its ability to sustain the wealth created and to create more. Favourable resource endowments, accessibility of technological know-how, availability of capital, reinforced this. The impact and scope of economic liberalisation has gradually percolated to all levels today. It has brought not only an understanding of the potentialities and possibilities of development but also an awareness of the ineffective initiatives taken earlier.

Just as economic indicators are important, so are the conditions, problems and dilemma that afflict the common people. These are the hidden indicators that reflect social accommodation and level of expectation. Failures to address to these issues despite electoral commitments and planned transition have left much to be desired of the development initiatives. Responses remained veiled and were expressed in terms of political discontent and mobilisation as a counter to increasing frustration and unemployment. Besides, located in the geopolitically sensitive region, experiments in economic development have introduced negative trends.

Optimistically, today, development can be telescoped, and economic indicators can be strengthened. But these require certain basic prerequisites essential for breaking the status quo. This also includes mass participation particularly that of Non-Governmental Organisations. These can act as a catalyst of change and introduce innovations in the field of development that otherwise would have been difficult in a society that is gradually transforming itself to a viable entity.

In this context, I have often discussed these issues in various academic gatherings. There were deliberations with other intellectuals, journalists, etc. I came across several observations but some of them became points of reference that called for careful consideration. These were capital/investment ratio, accessibility conditions, overall stability environment (which is linked with the region as a whole), fruitation of development priorities and appropriate policy initiatives and implementation and so on. These exercises also made it clear that Meghalaya had favourable endowments which needed only an appropriate direction and thrust. This over a period of time will go a long way in ensuring improvements in material life conditions of the common people. As of now, concentration of service-based development in urban and administrative nodes of the state have hidden the real agenda of much needed improvements in agriculture and rural economy in the state Indicators like purchasing power parity clearly indicate significant variations. For the purposes of studies, complex models have been used and debated and used as indices of human development. These presented only certain facets of living conditions. These statistics do not indicate the long-term sustainability of the quality of life achieved by people.

Terms like Globalisation and Economic Liberalisation, at a broader level, mean integration with and influence of the world economy into our society. Some opine that these are largely economic or market forces, but agree that they have beneficial influence in developing the core competencies in which the state has comparative advantage. These scholars also suggest that competition, both internally and with other players would be useful to make the state efficient and economically vibrant. But barriers that sap the development initiatives often plague these. Issues are closely intertwined with many aspects of commerce, investment as well as creation and use of a knowledge base. The state has to realise these new realities. This does not mean the advocacy of isolation or restrictions. One needs to address newer and more sophisticated concepts of protecting interests.

Such development initiatives then would include an effort to expand the domestic market, expansion of the wage economy, encouraging self-employment and expanding informal economy despite growth of formal sector. These need to be complimented by simultaneous growth of production and service sectors. It also calls for modernisation of agriculture and qualitative transition in the rural economy as well as introduction of agro-climatic conducive economic activities. Besides, calling for substantial increase in small and medium entrepreneurship with technocrats /professionals leading entrepreneurship. Some of the natural assets like that of the tourism potential needs to be exploited to supplement the efforts and perhaps induce more interactions in other fields of the economy. In general, these involve massive exercises of integrating the various sectors, their potentials, priorities and the their translation into reality. The need for both short-term and long-term perspectives requires be appreciating and implementing in tandem. Fruition of efforts provides the needed optimism and hope that fuels further effort in this direction.

The later aspect is pursued vigorously by other states in the country. And, in order to not to be left behind, political leadership in Meghalaya has identified policies of industrial resurgence to improve the economy through competition. This paradigm shift, has brought about optimism that Meghalaya, through these initiatives, the state will emerge as one of the most industrialised states in the country, let alone the North-Eastern region. Some of the sectors that have been initially identified involve the fields of environment friendly activities like horticulture, pharmaceuticals, steel fabrication, cement and so on. Efforts have also been geared to attract investments with some success. Nodal points such as Lumgshong in the east near the Cachar-Jaintia border for cement and Nangalbibra and Myntdu for power projects, are some that have been identified in this direction.

There is also a healthy optimism that Meghalaya, as compared to other states in the region, was in a better position to provide necessary infrastructure facilities. These alongwith measures to improve the state's resources of coal and limestone were expected to provide a launching pad for economic take off. There is no doubt that such positive initiatives are necessary and need to be pursued with single-minded commitment. It also requires careful consideration of factors that tend to introduce inertia and stagnation. Over and above, there is a necessity to evolve a political consensus as to the economic priorities of the state. A greater transparency in priorities and implementation will pave way for more effective visible impact of these efforts. It, then, will induce the society to debate and accept the fruits of such efforts. In order to bring transformation, it is imperative to recognise that technology and mass participation are the tools that bring faster economic growth. The absence of greater technological impetus has led to lower productivity and wastage of resources. Activities with low productivity or low value addition, in the final analysis, have perhaps forced stagnation.

Thus, looking at people, economy, and ability to sustain and improve on these over very long periods of time in the future, it would appear that mastering of technology and consensus on economic priorities among the major participants of development are the key tasks to which the state has to give importance. This can be considered to be the very essence of development. It is in this framework of understanding that Professor R.C. Sharma (Visiting Professor, Nagaland University, Lumami Campus, and Mokokchung Nagaland) with more than three decades of experience in the Northeast, delivered his inaugural address. This is reproduced below.

Involving People in the Development at the Grass-roots Level—Some Ideas

Prof. R.C. Sharma
Guest Professor

In post-independence India, very important experiences have been acquired with the process of development planning and as a result there has been frequent paradigm changes, perhaps for better results. Presently, the buzzwords are 'grass-roots planning' 'mobilization of resources' and the 'sustainable development' With all this, it is the question of people's involvement and the paramount importance of the non-governmental organization. No body has the doubt about the efficacy of such an approach, when one considers the best input-output development framework in a country with huge manpower potentials and scarcity of other necessary inputs. It has assumed paramount importance when the emphasis is on the questions and the processes of micro-level development planning and on the questions of watershed development planning covering a multitudinal framework, where the role of the local communities becomes essential. If one takes a critical over-view of the various committees appointed by the Planning Commission of India, it becomes very evident that the Sixth Five Years Plan and afterwards, the local level planning has been over-arching in emphasizing the importance of the peoples' involvement. It has become further important with a pertinent focus on self-sustaining development, which calls for the participation of the poor at the local level.

The development process is a mix of decision making, implementation process, monitoring and sharing of benefits, and this can become possibly ideal, if there is significant peoples involvement, that too, voluntarily and with greater amount of willingness. All this is the sine qua non of the bottom-up approach, which call for the confidence building measures at the local level development planning.

Syndrome, especially in the case of developing countries, where the poverty is deeply entrenched and the fruits of planned development are highly skewed in favour of the rich sections of the societies.

As a necessary framework for sustainable development, it is the prime question of involving the non-governmental organisations (NG0s), because the experience about the planned development by the government says that it cannot fully deliver the desired development change. In the case of India, there is a past record of successful functioning of such organisations, especially in the field of educational, cultural and social development. The state of Bengal can boost of a rich heritage, where Atmiya Sam (1815) and Ram Krishan Mission played very crucial role in spreading education and in eradicating many prevailing social ills of the society. Such initiatives are not only confined to Bengal but one come across equally very important and active organisations in India,e.g. Friend-in-Need Society (Madras 1858), Servants of India Society (1905), Servants of Peoples Society (1921) and others like Brahma Samaj, Arya Samaj and Christian Missionaries etc. Mahatma Gandhi came on the scene and set up very important organisations like Khadi and Village Industries Association, All Indian Spinners Association (1925) and such traditions continued with eminent personalities of India like Vinoba Bhave's Sarvodaya Movement and Jaya Prakash Narain Movement. On occasions of serious natural calamities due to floods, famines and earthquakes numerous people's organisations played important role.

The history, the heritage and inherent ethos of the Indian society has provided great impetus to the people's role in building up communities in different part of the country. During the 60's and 70's there has been mushrooming of the non-governmental organizations of different shades and character, some genuine and many non-genuine in nature. There is almost a flooding. The North-Eastern Region of India has not legged behind A cursory glance on the list of such organizations adds to the very fact that hundreds of such NG0s exist in small states like

Meghalaya, Manipur, Mizoram, Nagaland and Arunachal Pradesh. The large state like Assam is having NG0s in thousands. Seeing their records, some exist just for namesake, others are moneymaking shops and others with political motivations for their existence. However, some have achieved remarkable success, some have not done what they were aiming at on account of shortage of funding. and some faced difficulties of varying character and therefore remained dormant.

Besides the above characteristics and accompanied difficulties the NGO's specially in the tribal regions such as in Meghalaya have lack of leadership, profound state of confusion and no proper vision to locate the correct source of funding. The present workshop has revealed this state of affair. A close and intimate dialogue with many of the responsible functionaries of the registered NG0s has invariably disclosed this state of affair and their functional inability, in spite of the best commitment on their part. It has resulted not only in circumscribed action-fields but has dampened their ethos and enthusiasm to develop the localities where they are active and committed to bring a desirable change in the quality of life and the living environment. They feel disappointed and are on the verge of collapse. However, there is no dearth of zeal and motivation. Therefore, it is a happy state of affair and one can expect something nice, and constructive in bringing up the desired transformation.

Organisationally, in the state of Meghalaya specially but generally in the case of the North-East, what is essentially required is some concrete framework, for example:

The state needs functionally knit together block-to-district and district-to-state level information systems which collect, disseminate and debate and dialogue on the various aspects of schemes sponsored by the government at the state and national levels as well as by the international agencies.

The documentation centres need to be set up, may be operated by the representative NGOs in the area, to enable the NGOs to update themselves as well as provide free access to prescribed formats and guidelines for approaching the agencies for funding as well as networking with the organisations within or outside the country; the create necessary linkages for educating themselves through occasional professional visits to other places where very successful NGOs have achieved great success; and finally, there should he regular state-level meetings and workshops to review, monitor the future action-oriented programmes of the NGOs and working association with the various line-departments engaged in the task of rural development in the state.

This means the role of the state government at the block-level, district-level and the state level is of utmost importance, not only in guiding the NGOs but keeping them in liaison with the state machinery. This will provide a very close partnership framework, which has been completely lacking. Here it is also important to note that the North-Eastern Council (NEC) is overall in-charge of developing proper ethos and framework in the North-Eastern Region as well as in effacing marked disparities in the level of living. It is very evident that the NEC has pumped in huge financial inputs but the desired level of gains are not achieved, probably, NEC has always acted as an organisation heavily dominated by the elites from politics and administration and has never substantially engineered the people dialogue and participation. Therefore, it is necessary that the NEC should come down to interact regularly with the NGOs of the region and should develop a necessary institutional framework for interaction and dialogue with the NGOs of the region through regular meetings and constant feeding in of the information. Perhaps, if there is no apex body to achieve these ends at the regional level, the North-Eastern Council should urgently initiate such a step to fill up these lacunae. It is not out of the place to make a note that the CAPART with its North-East headquarter at Guwahati may take a lead in generating. proper development ethos by bringing up functional linkages between the NGOs and the Government. The role of the media is to be streamlined through the dialogue created by the "Regional Think Tank". If such a think tank does not exist, then the development specialists, technocrats and intellectuals of the region should generate it.

The North-Eastern Region abounds with resources as well as the developmental imbalances and ultimately the picture is dismal and calls for urgent attention and new framework. There has been peoples' apathy but the contemporary scene has abundance of enthusiasm for development and better quality of life. The people are fully motivated but what they required is necessary orientation and guidelines. The task is stupendous and cannot he achieve single-handedly by the government, therefore, a mix of governmental and non-governmental efforts is of paramount importance. This will provide a viable alternative model for development, ensuring the grassroots development planning and development and sharing of development gains. This will be the self-sustaining development for better quality of life and the safe-living environment.

Chapter II

Summary Report of the Workshop entitled Voluntary Organisations and Sustainable Rural Development, held between 27th and 29th June 2000 at Youth Hostel, Shillong

Nearly 80 NGOs/VO's, out of which 33 were from urban areas, participated in the workshop. The workshop was inaugurated by Prof. R.C. Sharma, retd. Prof. of JNU, New Delhi and at present Visiting Professor of Geography at Nagaland University. His inaugural speech set the trend for subsequent discussion in the workshop. These trends were: ability of the NGOs to come out with an honest opinion about themselves and the objectives which each one had set for themselves and ability of the NGOs/VOs to access the available economic opportunities and direct efforts towards meaningful, result-oriented programmes. The workshop included an inaugural session, a closing session and four technical sessions.

80 participating NGOs/VOs were divided into seven working groups to facilitate a meaningful interaction between them. They identified their respective group's strength, weakness, expectations and their future plans and programmes. These were discussed extensively. The Chairperson of the Social Welfare Board, Ministry of Social Welfare, Government of Meghalaya also addressed the workshop along with Mr. K.B. Rani, Assistant Director, CAPART, Regional Committee, North East Zone, and Guwahati. Interest on the Workshop was also shown by NEC, Shillong, Nehru Yuvak Kendra, Shillong and Voluntary Action Network India (VAN), New Delhi. There was full attendance in all the sessions of the

workshop. Participating NGOs/VOs were full of enthusiasm. They appreciated the efforts of the organisers in acquainting them with information that will facilitate and improve the functions as NGOs.

From PANACEA's point of view, the salient features of the workshop can be summarised as follows:

a. The workshop has been received with tremendous enthusiasm. This is clearly evident from the active participation of 80 NGOs/VOs. They also maintained full attendance in all the sessions.They effectively interacted both with the resource persons as well as among themselves.
b. This enthusiasm was also evident from the presence of the NEC representatives, particularly on the first day of the workshop, who collected the list of participating NGOs and VOs.
c. The Chairperson of the Social Welfare Board of the Govt. of Meghalaya, Mrs. T. Phanbuh addressed the third session (1000–1300 hrs, 28 June). She acquainted the NGOs with various plans and programmes of the state administration and provided them with details of schemes and programmes initiated by the state in this direction.
d. Mr. K.B. Rani, Asst. Director, addressed the NGOs and provided them with the details of CAPART programmes and schemes and the way in which the NGOs could seek CAPART assistance. He also provide the necessary details.
e. Nehru Yuva Kendra, Shillong also extended Rs. 15000/- each for interested NGOS as one-time assistance for stationery requirements.
f. A representative of the Voluntary Action Network India, New Delhi, also distributed relevant literature to the participating NGO's.
g. The NGOs identified 17 priorities. These were subsequently presented at the closing function held on 29th June 2000. These included aspects such as a need to develop unity and cooperation among various NGO's, the need to develop and promote tourism, the need to enforce accountability, community leadership, self reliance etc., to create an understanding of a viable action plan to facilitate training, strengthen financial base of NGO's for carrying developmental work, to encourage growth of meaningful vocational education, community based health centers, etc. The NGOs also emphasized upon the importance of information technology, whose presence in the area is negligible.

h. Efforts are being made to publicize the results of this workshop in local print and electronic media at the first instance, local newspapers like Aphira and The Meghalaya Guardian came out with reports on the workshop. Other Newspapers are likely to print the abstract of the proceedings. There were representatives of DD and AIR. DD televised the proceedings of the workshop in their CITYSCAN programme on 28th June.
i. Complete accounts and statements of expenditure incurred in the workshop will be submitted to CAPART, Regional Committee, North East Zone, and Guwahati. Mr. K.B. Rani Asst. Director, CAPART, Guwahati, promised to immediately reimburse the same.

The workshop has been able to achieve the following:

1. It has been able to create awareness among the NGOS about their sources of finance, their function and their role as a catalyst in development of the state.
2. The workshop was also able to enhance awareness of the need for interaction among and between the NGO's as well as coordinate developmental efforts. The need to sustain interest was accepted and was to be achieved through strengthening the training aspects, infusion of suitable and appropriate technology and skills that could ensure benefit of the core group.
3. Workshop also recognised the role of PANACEA as a facilitator. It proposed efforts to be directed by Panacea to introduce the NGOs to various funding organizations and create conditions by which suitable initiatives can be introduced in the areas where the NGOS operate. This was to be achieved through distribution of the final report of the Workshop.
4. Follow-up actions have been identified. PANACEA plans to publish the proceedings of the workshop. It will also submit a project proposal to CAPART. This will involve the NGOs that participated in the workshop.
5. Efforts will be made to bring in sponsors for development projects where PANACEA will monitor the implementation of such projects by keeping the agencies informed.
6. There were significant obstacles in the conduct of the workshop. These were largely in terms of last minute regret by resource persons and guests. The participants themselves who presented their views on the three days of workshop proceed-

ings overcame these. In short, these views appreciated the efforts of PANACEA to acquaint the NGOs with their role in development as well as sources for financial, technical and management assistance.

Methodology adopted in the workshop

Prof. R.C. Sharma, Father K. Paul,and Dr. A.K. Nongkinrih divided various participants into 6 groups.: these were:-

1. West Khasi Hills — Group I
2. East Khasi Hills — Group II
3. Jaintia Hills — Group III
4. Ri Bhoi district — Group IV
5. Shillong — Group V
6. Sohra Sub Division — Group VI

All the group was assigned to elect their Chairman and Secretary for better functioning. Each of such group carried out the SWOT Analysis on the District and NGO's.

These were subsequently followed by address to the participants by Mrs. Theilin Phanbuh, Chairman, Meghalaya State Social Welfare Advisory Board, Shillong, and the General Secretary, Ka Lympung Ki Seng Kynthei, Shillong. Both these speakers explained the various schemes available for the NGOs. These were summed up as to include—

(1) Rural Schemes which deals with environment, health, education etc.
(2) Women, child and disabled person scheme.
(3) Awareness Programme to cover especially the place where ICDS had not gone.
(4) The scheme for creche.
(5) A scheme for confidence school of education.
(6) Skilled improvement schemes.
(7) Vocational training for women.
(8) Socio-economic programme
(9) Working women hostel
(10) Short stay home.

Mr. Lakador Syiem added to the discussiopn by stating that VHAM has got a provision for Training on Basic Data Collection.

Since to start any developmental work survey is needed and it involve certain technique to do it, so VHAM can help in providing technique for survey.

Mr. K.B. Rani Asstt. Director, CAPART, NE Zone Guwahati, also confirmed that the exercise of the SWOT Analysis was encouraged by his organistaion (since CAPART also wanted the NGOs to about the local level planning process, participation, etc.)

Mr. Rani stated that there were 3 schemes available at present which can cater to the needs of rural development.

(1) Public cooperation (PC)—This schemes cover all project which can bring public cooperation.
(2) Organisational of Beneficiaries (OB)—This schemes to make the beneficiaries understand the benefits of being together.
(3) Rural Technology (RT)—This scheme cover all technology relating to rural development there is also a demonstration project to check whether it will work in the rural areas.

Group 1

Dist.: West Khasi Hills

Strength

1. Largest district in Meghalaya
2. Availability of natural resource (uranium etc.)
3. Presence of many tourism sport
4. Rich in forest resources
5. Good roads for transportation and good markets
6. Availability of hospitals, schools
7. Presence of different religious group
8. Responsible administrators
9. Strong culture
10. Co-operation among the people
11. Financially strong business man
12. Presence of Govt. offices
13. Presence of strong NGO's

Weakness

1. Lack of co-operation
2. Lack of communication facilities, media, roads

3. Lack of Govt. offices in the district and health center
4. Lack of Educational institute and training centre, marketing and industries
5. Lack of skill among the farmers
6. Too much dependency on timber trade
7. Supporstition

Opportunities

1. Self employment
2. Vocational training
3. Communication
4. Tourism
5. Hydro project
6. Mineral resources
7. Forest products
8. Agriculture and livestock
9. Education
10. Sericulture and weaving
11. Job oriented education

Problems/inadequacies

1. Lack of trained Medical Officers in various fields
2. Increased in the number of youths engaged in immoral activities
3. Rice of alcohol Abuse
4. Rise of number of unemployed
5. Religious conflicts
6. Rise in the number of anti social activities
7. Corruption
8. Environmental degradation
9. Lack of knowledge of farmers to used fertilizers etc.
10. Dishonest politician
11. Danger from uranium mining.
12. Migration from outside the state, Nation

Strength: NGO

1. Efficient leadership and co-operation among the members
2. Proper finacal assistance
3. Efficient administration

4. Co-operation among the NGO's, Govt. and the community
5. Co-operation and support from the general public

Weakness

1. Lack of efficient leader, member etc.
2. Lack of trust
3. Lack of youth centers
4. Dictatorship by the Executive Member.
5. Lack of understanding between the NGO's and people
6. Misguided

Opportunity

1. Active participation of NGO's in giving training
2. NGO's take active part in Developing the region
3. NGO's keep the people to understand better working of the government
4. NGO's also serve as bodies to safe guard the right of the people
5. Government schemes of the NGO's

Problems/inadequacies

1. Misused of the organisation for other purposes
2. Increased in the number in efficient organisation
3. Jealousy
4. Lack of understanding

Group 2

District: East Khasi Hills

Strength

1. Centrally located
2. Good transport and communication facilities
3. Educational and marketing centre
4. High literacy rate
5. Better standard of living
6. Availability of Natural Resources
7. Rich in Agricultural product and forest resources

8. High potentiality for tourism
9. The presence of traditional chief

Weakness

1. Political conflict, communal conflict and man made calamities.
2. Lack of trained staff, transparency and accountability
3. Lack of awareness programmes in rural area by youth, Deptt. (office) and trained staff in certain Govt. Deptt.
4. Lack of formalities in Govt. schemes
5. Irregularities of doctors and standard of education in Rural area
6. Monopoly and irresponsibilites of bureaucrats
7. Negative interference by politician, misleading manifestation and law and order problem
8. Excessive use of Narcotic Drugs by youngsters and rapid spread of AIDS (HIV+)
9. Non-participation of women in decision making
10. Lack of job oriented courses
11. Migration of population (rural to Urban)

Opportunity

1. Active women participation
2. Encouraging active participation of CGO's

Problems/inadequacies

1. Lack of preparation of responding to unilateral project which will have to negative impact on the purpose
2. Negative impact of Globalisation
3. Unequal—distribution of land
4. Wide income gap
5. High rate of drops out
6. Unemployment and Migrate labourers
7. Unscientific ways of farming/interacting, minerals, distruction of ecology and natural calamities
8. Border area of dispute and extinction of local culture

Strength—NGO's

1. Good support with the government
2. Democratic function

3. Emergence of enthusiastic social workers
4. Young and dynamic staff

Weakness

1. Lack of mission, goal and target
2. Lack of Net-working among NGO's and co-operation among member's and community
3. Lack of NGO's working in the field of development and community participating in development programme
4. Lack of legal awareness and information about various scheme
5. Lack of financial Assistance and proper document
6. Lack of bottom approach by various agencies and advocacy process with the Govt. policies

Opportunity

1. Positive initiative from the youth
2. Existing democrative set up

Problems/inadequacies

1. Negative respond even to responsible NGO's
2. Dependency of financial and technical support
3. Law and order situation
4. Rapid spread of HIV (AIDS)

Group 3

District: Jaintia Hills

Strength

1. Official of NGO's genrally elected from amongst good and anticidence members
2. Good and fair of NGO's
3. Lack of partiality
4. Quick disposal of different schemes as it was locally well conversant
5. Good soil for agriculture and horticulture
6. Border market
7. Mineral resources
8. Education

Weakness

1. Dictatorship and of officials
2. Lack of knowledge and education for main training official records and prepare project report in certain cases.
3. Financially weak institution cause a problem to move ahead
4. Acidity of soil/water
5. Deforestation
6. Illiteracy
7. Lack of schemes from government
8. Political favoritism

Opportunity

1. Co-operation amongst the NGO's
2. Availability of foreign aid when there is financial crunch of the government
3. Good climate condition
4. Transportation
5. Market improvement
6. Potential know how on modern technology.

Problems/inadequacies

1. Insincerity and dishonesty in management
2. Pessimistic views and opinions of the members discourage the success of NGO's
3. Selfishness of capitalist and towards the upliftment of rural poor people
4. Unemployment problem creates bad social elements
5. Inter-cross marriage effect the culture of Jaintia people
6. Rapid growth of population due to uncontrol of birth rate due to lack of education

Group 4

District: Ri Bhoi

Strength

1. Fertile soil
2. Moderate climate

3. Adequate rainfall
4. Forest wealth (timber)
5. Rich flora and Fauna
6. Minerals
7. Indegenious skills
8. Rich culture
9. Plenty of Electricity
10. Airport, road (communication)
11. Education centres (literacy)
12. Research and training centres
13. Industries

Weakness

1. Disease
2. No family planning and hygine
3. Illiteracy
4. Bad leadership
5. Outdate agriculture method
6. Buyers market
7. Lack of road communication
8. Lack of electrification
9. Environmental degradation
10. Land dispute
11. Border dispute (interstate)

Opportunities

1. Government developmental scheme
2. Youth development Scheme
3. Present of strong NGO's
4. Medicinal plant
5. Traditional cottage industry
6. Plantation crops
7. Crop protection skills

Problems/inadequacies

1. Outside influx
2. Rampart deforestation
3. Pollution

4. Lack of sanitary system
5. Insurgency
6. Ineffective administration (corruption)
7. Lack of career guidance
8. Social evil

Strength of NGO

1. Collective bargaining power
2. Able leadership and choice member
3. Strength of commitment
4. Understanding of local needs
5. Recognition of Govt. and funding agencies
6. Result oriented and effective
7. Transparency and Accounability

Weakness

1. Wrong choice of leaders
2. Financial weakness
3. Inconsistant staping power
4. Petty politics
5. Religious and political fanaticism

Opportunities

1. Availability of schemes
2. Close contact with people (trust)
3. Introduction of new technology
4. Participation of the people
5. Highlighting of social needs

Problems/inadequacies

1. Lack of trust (non co-operation) amongst members
2. Indiscipline (internal politics)
3. Lack of networking knowledge
4. Lack of commitment
5. Communal tension

Group 5

Shillong

Strength: NGO

1. Co-operation amongst the NGO's
2. Efficient administration
3. Self supporting
4. Capability of maintaining reports
5. Presence of efficient people in the organisation
6. New aware of the rule and reputation
7. Well aware of the people to approach for help

District

1. Being the capital of the state there are many advantages
2. Good educational institution
3. Availability of good roads and means of transportation and communication
4. Availability of plans for re-creation purpose
5. Presence of efficient administrators
6. Presence of many government offices
7. Availability of sufficient water resources

Weakness: NGO

1. Lack of transparency in financial matters
2. Jealousy among members
3. Different of opinion among members
4. Lack of communication skills
5. Members take part in politics
6. Enrolment of members to any organisation without scanning

Weakness (District)

1. Lack of co-operation and unity
2. Lack of peace
3. Lack of knowledge for encouraging development
4. Lack of transparency in various fields of work
5. Corruption in different fields of work
6. Unemployment problem due to lack of factories and industries

7. Lack of marketing facilities

Opportunity (NGO's)

1. Information through workshop and seminar
2. Opening up of vocational institute
3. Starting up of workshop
4. Availability of all round information
5. Self employment opportunities
6. Opening up of trading agencies

Opportunity (District)

1. Employment opportunity through travelling agencies
2. Setting up of marketing agencies
3. Setting up of small workshops

Problems

1. Rise in the numbers of NGO's and pressure groups
2. Lack of peace
3. Lack of understanding among the NGO's and the pressure groups
4. Corruption
5. Misuse of the organisation for selfish motives

Inadequacies

1. Water pollution
2. Migration of people to Shillong both from the rural areas and people from other states
3. Lack of cleanliness
4. Corruption
5. Air pollution
6. Deforestation
7. Lack of peace
8. Unemployment
9. Misuse of power by Govt. Officials
10. Immoral activities
11. Negligence of traditional culture

Group 6

District: Sohra Civil Sub-division

Strength

1. Availability of cement factory, government offices and small scale industries
2. Availability of marketing facilities and border trade
3. Availability of school, colleges
4. Moderate climate
5. Distingtive trees
6. Availability of medicinal plants (Hervs) and raw materials
7. There are different types of festivals
8. There are fresh air, clean water and abandoned rainfall
9. Hereditary policy
10. Democratic policy in India
11. Free franchise of people in the election
12. Availability of representatives like the MLA/MDC, headman, syiemship etc.

Weakness

1. Lack of Market facilities
2. Lack of small scale industries
3. Lack of local people working in Govt. offices at Sohra
4. Unauthorised excavation of underground minerals
5. The Govt. does not take interest for introducing self-employment relating to finish products
6. No pollution control and lack of transportation
7. Lack of professional teachers in schools and colleges
8. Irresponsibilities of teachers
9. Lack of Non-formal School/Vocational Training
10. There are villages with no existance of school
11. Teachers do not et adequate payment/salary
12. Malnutrition and unhygenic living
13. Clash of religion and fanatic religious people

Opportunities

1. To develop the market facilities and border trade
2. To develop the tourism like hotels, guide, tourist spots etc.

3. To select some places to convert as an industrial estate
4. People are eager for learning
5. Setting of nigh schools and training centres
6. There are fertilise soil for cultivation
7. Trees can be planted anywhere
8. Air and Water pollution can be prevented by new technology
9. There are so many places which attrated the tourist
10. Hydel project dam can be constructed
11. Health centres can be increases in number and size

Problems/inadequacies

1. Unemployment will leads youths to anti social activities
2. Markets in the areas will low down
3. Destroy of forest by a fire will turn Sohra into a land of desert
4. If there is no trees the source of water will be exhausted
5. Unscientific excavation of underground Minerals will make the hilly areas collapsed
6. Animals and Medicinal herbs will extinct

Strength: NGO

1. Availability of NGO's in greater number
2. People are working together and taking parts of youths in social work
3. Increasing number of women in education and availability of vocational training institution
4. Togetherness of people during problems and their religious belief (Earn with Honesty)
5. There are plenty of vegetables, fruits and food
6. People belief in their own religion and it helps the development of the knowledge and the society

Weakness of NGO's

1. Farming have not been started
2. Lack of encourgement from the elders and small number of women working in social work
3. No opportunity for rural people working for the society
4. Alcoholism, early marriage and divorce
5. Leaving schools without finishing it
6. No participation of people in cultural programme

Opportunities

1. To get their own district (South Khsi hills district)
2. The areas are suitable for culture and
3. We can establish any social organisation
4. People are accepting the programmes of the NGO's
5. To unite and maintain the culture and tradition of the people
6. Can organise any Health awareness programme for rural people
7. There are many intelligent leaders if the people know how to choose them

Problems/inadequacies

1. Air and water pollution can cause many diseases
2. Women will be higher in education
3. Greater number of Men who left school without finishing it can create unemployment
4. Availability of uneducated leaders can be dangerous in the policy of working
5. Lack of sanitation and Health centres

Recommendation for NGO's

1. NGO's must implement Govt. sponsored schemes with sincerity
2. NGO's working in rural areas must unit
3. NGO's must sensitized the community on the importance of economic gains of tourism
4. NGO's must be responsible, transparent and accountable to the community
5. NGO's must consult the community relating to leadership
6. NGO's must teach the people to be self employed
7. NGO's must have a clear understanding on the vision, mission and action plan
8. NGO's must facilitate training of staff
9. NGO's must strengthen financial management
10. NGO's must seek the help of guidance of experts of different fields to assist them in their work
11. NGO's must organise awareness programmes
12. NGO's must faciliated skill training in different fields
13. NGO's must promote a faciliated income generating activities
14. NGO's must promote education

15. NGO's must promote and facilitated community based health centers
16. NGO's must promote facilitate a work for the empowerment of marginised womens
17. To take advantage of Information Technology

Recommendation for the administration

1. Promoting agriculture and intensive training for villagers
2. Promoting and supporting record unit based industry
3. Building of infrastructure (Road, Communication, Electrical)
4. Promoting and supporting developmental base NGO's
5. Promoting and supporting tourism through NGO's SHG's, CBO's
6. To open a separate cell for give child and also a separate court
7. To provide basic education to children below 14 yrs. of age especially street children
8. Public schools must cater to the marginalised children
9. All Govt. deptt. must provide all public information of all the Govt. schemes
10. To provide training in modern technology
11. To build fisheries college
12. To promote and encourage handicraft
13. To create special schemes for the illiterate and the dropout's
14. To facilitate marketing facilities
15. To chanalise development schemes in the rural areas through NGO's CBO'S SHG'o and co-operative societies
16. Govt. must create a separate cell which is meant only for NGO's SHG'S and CBO'o
17. Govt. must facilitate information technology

Suggestion for CAPART

1. CAPART must give wide publicity to its Scheme by publishing in the Newspapers etc.
2. CAPART must provide personal assistance for project formulation

Expectations from the Workshop Organised by Panacea and the participants also suggested the fofllowing:

Strength of the Organisation

- Has a secular and democratic board members
- Qualified Executive members
- Good reporting system
- Capacity leadership
- Net working system with NGO and Government agencies
- Young motivated and committed staff
- Having its own training centre (Workshop)
- Self sufficient
- Work for marginalise group
- Welfare activities for the disable person
- Trained leader
- Better organisational management
- Having their own land and office
- Health management

Weakness of the Organisation

- Lack of financial assistance
- Lack of marketing facilities
- Lack of administration management
- Lack of linkage system with like minded NGO and Government
- Lack of proper knowledge about the concept of development
- Communication gap
- Lack of co-operation among the members
- Lack of man power
- Disaster management
- Less advance skill on management
- Internal resource mobilisation
- Lack of transparency and accountability

Expectations of the Organisation

- Quality management in development sector
- Linkage with government agencies and like minded NGO's
- To acquire more knowledge about the NGO's sector

- Fund mobilisation
- Problem identification
- Technical guidance
- Administration, financial, staff and modern management
- Leadership training

Future Programmes of the Organisation

- Setting upon integrated resource centre for the youth
- Enlarging the vocational training centre
- Strengthen of Development programme
- Staff exposure trip (Tour)
- Skill training in livestock and agriculture management
- Conceptual skill management
- Project writing and assessment
- Ensure liaison with the bank for soft loan and act as guarantor for the project
- Enterpreneurship development programme
- To promote the concept of saving
- Promotion of SHG
- To prepare action plan
- Setting up of a rural health centre, creach and women vocational training centre

CHAPTER III

Sustainable Development: The PANACEA Approach

From the 1950s through the 1970s and 1990s, the economy of the Northeastern region has undergone several changes. These were neither conducive to encourage growth and thus sustain development activities nor did it enable the region to be in a position to meet and address the expectations and requirements of the regional society. This was contrary to the certainty and the optimism that characterised the initiation of the planned economic transition.

In retrospect, hopes were belied and perhaps, shattered as it became increasingly difficult to realize the planned economic objectives for both the region as a whole in general and the constituent states in particular. The expansion of public sectors in the states of the region after the consolidation and administrative reorganization has been disproportionate in terms of allocation to increase economic opportunities. However, as the rate of economic growth declined in the successive decades, the result was a growing concern about the capacity of a welfare state to deliver. Governments in the region have faced serious economic predicaments. Economic problems worsened even though or maybe *because* respective governments, over time, accumulated huge deficits to pay for a sustained expansion of the administrative structure.

Consequently, one can argue that besides those with geopolitical undertones, the reasons for instability in the region have been mainly economic ones. Frequent bandhs, curfews and strikes, economic blockades, and so on,—all have become characteristic features of the Northeast today. This is not to argue such disruptions do not occur elsewhere in the country. It is only suggested that with a fairly developed economic base, such disruptions cause minimal impact, and do not assume social and political ramifications as it has emerged in the North East.

Such disruptions at the cost of economy and the general welfare of the society, normally invokes substantial public response. But the scale of discontent that came to be expressed in the closing decades of the twentieth century in the region suggests combination of factors that emerged as catalyst for under developed status of the region today.

The North-East is a region of varied cultures, peoples and ethnic groups. Lack of adequate infrastructure, continuing impact of locational inertia, inadequate economic base and absence of effective accessibility and communication linkages, to name a few, have been responsible for the existing status and the prime reason why people here still adhere to their small world view resulting in ethnic clashes and secessionist movements from time to time. This very reason has also led to some sort of a paranoia- immigration of people from outside the state, particularly from what we can call mainstream India, is seen as a threat to local tribal and ethnic identity. Hence the resistance towards developmental efforts like laying down of railway tracks and so on. The problem in this case is twofold: ethnic groups are at loggerheads with one another, on the one hand, as well as being pitted against the state on the other. To some extent, this can be attributed to the ineffectiveness of the state to improve prevailing circumstances, which has led to loss of faith in the state as an institution.. Political decision-making systems have barely served the interests of the people. At best, they have served to further narrow political interest based on tribal or ethnic loyalty. Secondly, people of this region see themselves as isolated from mainstream India-economically, culturally or otherwise.

A new phenomenon in regional politics was the emergence of social disorder that threatened vital state functions frequently leading to disruption of ongoing political activities. It was believed that insurgency had its roots in the law and order dimension, but it now becomes clear that not only bloodshed and continuous instability are possible in these societies, but that it may prove difficult even for states with large military resources to put an end to the operations of insurgents and urban guerrillas.

The region has witnessed violent changes that refused to accept accommodation and adjustment. Powerful tides of change created a bewildering variety of environments such as insurgency and terrorism, which worked at cross-purposes with one another. As a result, the regional economies floundered and there are instances where even the existing bare infrastructure facilities were marginalised. Ratings of the political fora and political groups plummeted. Let us take the example of Meghalaya.

With its level of economic development and complex social and political linkages, the state is faced with immense challenges. Its resolution has become more of a necessity and a compulsion rather than a mere initiative. However, the difficulties of the state have been mostly on the political arena that have outstripped progress on the economic and to some extent, the cultural arena. This has brought about a situation where the state's politics and economy are perpetually falling out of gear. On the political plane, it has remained fragmented, with political fora being founded on ethnic lines. This parochialism is reflected in the economy, in the articulation of interests and the concentration of funds and effort towards the satiation of those interests which are, more often than not, antithetical and consequently result in a series of jolts, clashes and jars in the economic and social life of the local populace. This situation , more or less repeats itself in the remaining states of the northeast.

PANACEA or Policy Alternatives for the Northeast and Conflict Elimination Awareness, as a solution to all of the above, is a Non-Governmental Organisation that reflects the concern to protect, preserve and accelerate measures to resolve the political and consequently the economic problems that have had a far-reaching impact on society. In a sense, such themes involve an accounting of how far and how well the awareness of problems have advanced and percolated to different levels of society and how well these were articulated by various political for a that represented the interests of society.

PANACEA seeks to identify and articulate the aforesaid problems and offers alternative measures, using the help of governmental and non-governmental agencies to achieve its objectives. It focuses upon cleavages, social and economic environments, decision-making mechanisms and political stability to show how complex these phenomena are. Empirical research on the region may present specific knowledge of how different factors influence stability in the region. One aim is to present a comprehensive assessment and understanding of the northeast region and while doing so, present viable alternatives that may be *useful* in formulation and implementation. First and foremost would be to analyze the causes of disaffection among the people and identify the problems that have led to such a situation in the northeast. Keeping the cultural diversity in mind, PANACEA also aims to promote an attitude of tolerance based upon an understanding of this diversity and the need for coexistence. Lastly, PANACEA aims at identifying major trends in social, economic and political development and formulation of suitable strategies towards sustained development and conflict resolution in the northeast.

Conclusion

Sustainable development is an expression of the awareness of the fact that we, as responsible citizens of our city, state, country and planet, must utilise our resources such that the needs of all interest groups are satisfied, at the same time ensuring that these resources are adequately replenished for use by future generations. This is the spirit of sustainable development: the acceptance that we live in an earth that we bequeath to our successors on this planet. This includes an entire action plan ranging from conservation of bio-diversity to social forestry, rural development programmes, population control and above all, the generation of motivation among people that development can be brought about with their own sustained efforts. With this in mind, PANACEA aims to highlight the role of non-governmental organizations in development, apart from creating awareness among the general people about the region, This is not to be misconstrued as a lack of faith in the government. It has to be remembered that any sort of attempt at development without the people's support is bound to end in failure. NGOs are instrumental in that they stand for development by the people's initiative. This is also where the role of programmes like the Jawahar rozgar yojna become effective, since they attempt to bring about progress from within the masses. What is important today is the coordination of efforts between governmental and non- governmental agencies and within NGOs. This workshop aims at bringing about this kind of cooperation and maintaining it, along with which the other problems of the northeast can be kept in mind to usher in sustainable development.

List of Major Participating NGOs/VOs

1. Iai Treilang Multi-Purpose Co-Operative Society, Phlangwanroi, P.O. Mawsynram.
2. Snohlang Development Society, Lumsohphoh, Lower Mawprem, Shillong.
3. Villagers Rural Development and Cultural Organisation, PO Marbisu 793121
4. Synkhong Rympei Thymmai Development Society, Jylli Shop—Nongthymmai, Shillong.
5. Mawlaisyiem Welfare and Development Society, Mawlaisyiem, Myriaw Elaka PO. Markasa (via Nongstoin).
6. Khatar Shnong Social Organisation, Maraikaphan, Sohra.
7. Sohra Science Society, Cherrapunji.
8. Dalade Multi-Purpose Co-Operative Society, Sohra.
9. United Rural Development Society, Smit, via Shillong 793021
10. Tuber Welfare Organisation, Jowai.
11. Smit Youth Development Organisation, Smit.
12. Sohra Environment Society, Maraikaphon, Sohra 793111.
13. Sohra Tourism Society, Maraikaphon, Sohra 793111.
14. R.S. Lyngdoh Training Centre, Smit, P.O. Madanriting, Shillong.
15. J.S.. Nonghseh International Social Vision, Nongrim Hills, Laitumkhrah, Shillong.
16. Rice Society, Mawjrong.
17. Laitkseh Sports & Cultural Organisation, PO. Laitkesh, W. Khasi Hills.
18. Pingwait Sports Social & Cultural Club, PO.Kharang, Khasi Hills, Shillong.
19. Sohbar Development Society, Sohbarpunje, Mawkisyiem, Lower Cherra, East Khasi Hills.
20. Umpohliew Society, Pohkseh, Shillong.
21. Synjuk Seng Samla Shnong, Mawkhar, Shillong.

22. Seng Samla Khlieh Shnong, Malki, Shillong.
23. Ri Bhoi Area Welfare Association, Umsning.
24. Sohra Rural Youth Development Centre, Makalkaphon, Cherrapunji.
25. Lait-Ryngew, Cherrapunji.
26. Sohra Rin Development Society, Sohra Rim, Cherrapunji.
27. Sohra Rural Youth Development Organisation, Cherrapunji.
28. Western Youth Welfare Organisation..
29. Ri-Bhoi Western Youth Welfare Organisation.
30. Ri-Bhoi Youth Federation.
31. Nam Rhen Association, Jaintia Hills.
32. Mr. Terrence Sawian and Mr Jeiborlang Hing of Jaintia Hills.
33. Umbir Youth-Ri Bhoi.
34. Kynthuplut Livestock Cooperative Society Jaintia Hills.
35. Mookian Cooperative Society, Jaintia Hills.
36. Mahgaram Youth Welfare Organisation.
37. Mr. Tony Blah, Coorodinator North-Eastern Region Community Resource Centre.

The NGOs are engaged in development activities in their respective areas for quite some time now. In their own way, these NGOs have channelised their respective efforts at the grass roots levels with fair measure of success. Through the workshop, it is proposed to identify and document the issues, problems and constraints of development in the predominantly hill areas.